About This Book

Matto H. Barfuss is a wildlife photographer and artist. On a trip to Serengeti National Park in Tanzania, Barfuss became fascinated by the graceful cheetah. After stumbling upon a family of wild cheetahs on the Serengeti, he decided to observe and photograph them in their natural environment. *My Cheetah Family* documents for the first time Matto Barfuss's extraordinary adventure watching, photographing, and living among a very special family of cheetahs.

My Cheetah Family

My Cheetah Family

Matto H. Barfuss

Carolrhoda Books, Inc./Minneapolis

Carolrhoda Books, Inc.
c/o the Lerner Publishing Group
241 First Avenue North
Minneapolis, MN 55401 U.S.A.
Website address: www.lernerbooks.com

LIBRARY OF CONGRESS CATALOGING-IN-PUBLICATION DATA

Barfuss, Matto H.
  [Meine Gepardenfamilie. English]
  My cheetah family / Matto H. Barfuss ;
[translated from the German by Amy Gelman
Haugesag]. – 1st North American ed.
     p.   cm.
  Includes bibliographical references (p.   ) and
index.
  Summary: A wildlife photographer describes
how he encountered a mother cheetah and her
five cubs in Serengeti National Park in Tanzania,
gained their trust, and photographed them over
a period of more than four months.
  ISBN 1-57505-377-2
  1. Cheetah–Tanzania–Serengeti National Park–
Juvenile literature. 2. Cheetah–Infancy–
Tanzania–Serengeti National Park–Juvenile
literature. 3. Serengeti National Park (Tanzania)
[1. Cheetah.] I. Title.
QL737.C23B26313 1999
599.75'9–dc21   98-33998

Printed in Italy by Editoriale Libraria, Trieste
Bound in the United States of America
1 2 3 4 5 6 – OS – 04 03 02 01 00 99

Contents

Opposite page: *This mother cheetah invited me into her den.*

Below: *My portrait of a cheetah*

How It All Began

I was visiting Serengeti National Park in Tanzania, in eastern Africa. I had been there several times before. But this time, everything was different.

Serengeti National Park is 5,600 square miles in size. It stretches about 120 miles from the south to the north and covers about 90 miles at its widest point.

Serengeti is a national park with strict rules. People come there only as guests. Otherwise, the park belongs to the animals: lions, cheetahs, leopards, elephants, rhinoceroses, giraffes, zebras, and many other small and large living things. They share an enchanted paradise.

It was June in the Serengeti. The dry season had begun. For weeks—usually until October—it would not rain. I drove across the plain and looked out on a vast sea of grass. In every direction only grass grows, higher in some places, lower in others. Only a few trees break the line of grass.

Suddenly, something in the distance caught my eye. I stopped and took a look through binoculars. An animal was sitting all alone on the plain. This was unusual, so I drove closer. I soon recognized the animal: It was a female cheetah. Slowly, I drove even closer. Cheetahs are very sensitive and are often afraid of cars and trucks. But this cheetah wasn't scared. And what a surprise! Behind the cheetah, five cubs lay in the grass. The mother had carefully hidden them. I waited until the cats got over the surprise of seeing me and my truck. The little ones slowly emerged from their hiding place. Giant eyes looked at me curiously.

I could tell that the cubs were eight to ten weeks old. They would soon be able to go with their mother on short trips across the plain. That would be a great relief to the female cheetah. She is responsible for raising the cubs. The father lives alone somewhere on the vast plain. The cheetah cubs never get to know him.

After birth, cheetah cubs are blind for five to ten days. But even after cubs open their eyes, it is some time before they leave their safe hiding place. This is a very dangerous time for the family. After all, the mother must nurse the always-hungry cubs. To have a constant supply of milk, she needs to eat regularly. Only after the female has carefully hidden her young and checked the area for dangers can she set off on the hunt.

The mother cheetah feeds the cubs. Five cubs often can't nurse at the same time. This causes fights among them.

The cubs wait patiently for her return. They must not cry or peek out of their hiding place, much less leave it. In the Serengeti, cheetah cubs have many enemies.

If the mother cheetah needs to travel far for food, or if her den is threatened by constant danger, the family has no other choice but to move. When this happens, the mother gently picks one of the cubs up by the neck, carries it to a new hiding place, and lays it in the grass. She quickly runs back and grabs the next cub, then the third, fourth, and fifth. It's a hard way to move a family. But it's better for the mother to know that her cubs are in a safe place, especially when she goes hunting.

From the truck, I watched the little family in their hiding place on the plain. I didn't move any closer, so as not to scare the mother and her cubs. It was getting dark. The mother cheetah found a protected place in medium-high grass for the night. She called her young with a clear, strong chirp. (Cheetahs don't meow or roar.) The cubs came along quickly and disappeared from view into the grass.

That cheetah family made such an impression on me that I decided I had to come back. I planned to watch them for just a few weeks. It turned out that I kept them company for four months. They became, in a way, my very own cheetah family.

Whenever the mother goes off, the young cheetahs watch her carefully.

Left: *When the mother goes hunting, she first hides her young. The little ones must not leave their hiding place for any reason. Otherwise, they may be discovered by enemies.*

Opposite page: *In the evening, the mother cheetah looks for a safe sleeping place.*

First Journeys

Each day, the cheetahs seemed to lose more of their fear of me and my truck. Soon, it no longer disturbed them when I drove up in the early mornings and followed them on short trips across the plain.

The mother cheetah watched her cubs closely. On trips, she would travel a few yards and then look back to make sure none of her young had fallen behind. The dry grass of the Serengeti is stiff and slows down young cats with their short legs. As soon as the little ones got tired, the mother made a rest stop.

If she saw a chance to hunt, her steps became faster. The little ones quickly gave up trying to follow her. They simply stayed in the grass and made themselves as big as possible so that they wouldn't lose sight of their mother. For what she was doing was very interesting to the growing cats.

If a mother cheetah is successful at the hunt, she calls her cubs to her. If they do not come running up quickly, she goes and gets them. She carries back any small dead animals in her jaws but leaves bigger ones behind for the moment.

Left: *A cheetah's strength is in its powerful legs, which help it take big leaps and run fast.*

Opposite page: *This cheetah cub is three months old. It tires quickly on journeys across the plain.*

World Speed Champions

Cubs walk clumsily, but they will grow up to be speedy runners. Cheetahs are the fastest land animals in the world. They reach speeds of up to 70 miles per hour. The cheetah's body is built for speed. Cheetahs move gracefully on long, powerful legs. When they run fast, their hind legs reach out in front of their front legs. Cheetahs can easily make leaps of nearly seven yards, one after another. Not even an Olympic-medal-winning human can do that.

At such high speeds, the cheetah relies on its long claws. Those claws dig into the soft soil of the plain and give the cat a good grip. Otherwise, the cheetah might lose its footing and be badly injured.

Cheetahs are the fastest animals on land. In fast bursts, they can reach speeds of up to 70 miles per hour.

Playing for Survival

Soon the young cheetahs were three months old. They still had a lot of training to do before they could run fast. In the coming weeks, they would gradually learn all kinds of skills from their mother. They watched her carefully, and then they had to try everything themselves.

Young cheetahs learn all the skills that are important in later life by imitating and by playing. In the cool morning and evening hours, the cubs chased each other around my truck or raced and tumbled through the grassy plain. Sometimes they joined in a big free-for-all. All the while, they raised giant clouds of dust in the dry grass that the wind carried away.

Later, more rules were added to the young cats' play. For example, roles were assigned. One cub was the hunter, the other played the prey animal, or the animal to be hunted. I watched one cub hide. It stared through the blades of grass at its brothers and sisters. But they didn't notice at all. They were looking in another direction. That's exactly what the young hunter was waiting for! It burst out of its hiding place and went after one of the cubs. The cub saw its attacker too late. The hunter leapt onto the back of its "victim," knocked it down, and gripped it softly by the throat.

Everything cheetahs need to know in later life they learn by watching their mother and by playing together.

Young cheetahs practice hunting. Usually one plays the hunter, the other a gazelle. The more skillful and swift cheetah will win.

Sometimes the cheetah cubs played too rough. Someone soon would get hurt, or someone would leave in a huff.

As soon as they get hot, the cheetah cubs stop playing and rest.

Even when the cubs were chasing each other, they were learning new skills. It's very important for the cheetahs to learn to use their tails. Cheetahs' tails are very long and powerful, helping them "steer" when running fast. The better they can use their tails, the more agile they will be. And the more agile they become, the more likely the cubs are to become successful hunters and survive on the Serengeti plain.

The First Hunt

When the cheetah cubs were five months old, a new period in their lives began. The family traveled farther across the plain. The cubs investigated everything they saw along the way.

Suddenly one day, a cheetah cub stopped and stood still. I could tell by the way it sniffed that there must be something there!

24

Left: *When the mother hunts, the cubs watch her every move.*

25

The cubs had watched their mother hunting many times. They had also played at hunting every day. Now they heard a rustling sound. A little gazelle leapt between clumps of grass. It was only a few hours old but could already run very fast. All the cheetah cubs immediately rushed after the baby gazelle.

Below: *The mother captures a rabbit.*

Just as they had while playing, the young hunters tried to trip the animal. And they succeeded. A good, strong grip on the throat would have ended the hunt. But even though the young cats had often watched their mother killing prey animals, it didn't work quite the same way for them. The gazelle didn't die quickly; it struggled on. In the end, all were exhausted, but the weary gazelle gave up.

The mother carefully observed the cubs' first hunting trip. She let the little hunters eat in peace. From now on, the cubs would use every opportunity to hunt on their own. They might not always manage to capture and kill their prey, but one day they would be just as skillful at hunting as their mother.

Below and opposite page, top: *The cheetah cubs chase a gazelle. They are hunting for the first time.*

Jealousy in the Family

After a hunt, my cheetah family seemed almost like a human family grabbing for "seconds." Each cub wanted to have the biggest share of food. The cats occasionally fought roughly. Even the mother fought to make sure she got a piece of the prey.

When the cheetah cubs are very hungry, they often fight over prey.

When the cheetah family had eaten enough, they quickly moved away from the carcass to a safe place. Carcasses often attract hyenas, which can attack young cheetahs. Once the cheetahs were in a safe place, the cats washed each other's coats in peace and rested. Hunting, eating, and washing are all hard work for cubs.

Left: *After the cheetahs have eaten their fill, they wash each other thoroughly with their tongues.*

29

Precious Water

The cheetah cubs were born during a dry season. The rains wouldn't return to the Serengeti until the end of October. Until the rains returned, the cheetahs used every opportunity to quench their thirst.

Sometimes cheetahs nibble on wet grass (above). *Very rarely, the family finds water in a rock crevice on the dry Serengeti* (below).

In the early mornings, they licked the dew from each other's coats. Or they nibbled on dew-drenched plants. Otherwise, they drank the blood of their prey. Only rarely did they find a bit of water in a rock crevice. Then the cheetahs' eager tongues didn't stop slurping until the precious water was gone.

Cheetahs love trees. It's too bad, then, that there are so few on the Serengeti plain. From a tree, cats can see clearly for several miles. Cheetahs have much better eyesight than humans. Their sharp eyesight helps them to choose a particular direction to travel. They can see dangers or prey animals from great distances.

Over the weeks, I became close friends with the cheetah family. Every morning when I arrived, they greeted me happily. In the evening, when I left, they even seemed a little bit sad.

The Truck as a Playground

At first, the cheetah family was surprised by my truck. But it soon became an interesting toy for them. The cubs had great fun play-hunting around or under it. Sometimes they even tried to jump up on the hood, but their claws couldn't grip the smooth finish. When they got bigger, the cubs would make a single bold leap onto the hood. Up there, they had a wonderful view. In the hottest time of day, if there was no tree or shrub nearby, they would sleep in the shade under my truck.

Once I got to know the family well, I began to leave one of the truck doors open now and then. That way the cheetah cubs could visit me. And since cheetahs are naturally very curious, the first cub soon came into the truck.

I saw in its big eyes how much it was intrigued by all the new things. It looked carefully and sniffed at everything. As soon as the cubs had spent some time with different parts of the truck, they got used to them and lost interest in them. Only the truck's windshield and windows held their interest. Again and again they pressed their noses against them.

My truck became a playground for the curious cheetah cubs.

Left and below: *Truck windows are confusing for the cheetahs.*

Occasionally, they tapped the panes with their paws. "Why can't we just go right through?" they seemed to ask.

Some days, the cheetah family invited me to visit them. Whenever I left the safety of the truck, I was *very* careful. Cheetahs are, after all, dangerous animals. I wanted to be very sure they were serious about their invitation. So first I would lie in the grass and wait until they approached. They would touch me with their paws and sniff me. Then I would follow them, but they would only let me visit if I walked on all fours.

The cheetahs feel safe on top of my truck. They have a wonderful view all around and can take a bite of windshield wiper.

The Little Ones Get Big

By December, the cheetah cubs were nine months old. Each day when they played, they played a little longer. It's a good thing that they had thick coats, because their claws had become long and sharp, and they could not pull them in fully.

The big cheetah cubs were hungrier. Their mother had a lot to do. She tried to hunt successfully every day. At the same time, she demanded a lot from her cubs.

The family traveled up to 18 miles in a day, always searching for prey animals. The cubs hunted everything that came their way. They also helped their mother watch for dangers. The cubs were old enough to take turns watching over each other. Finally their mother could sleep in peace, too!

The older the cheetahs get, the rougher their play becomes.

Left: *This cheetah cub has spotted gazelles in the distance.*

Opposite page: *Impalas and black-footed antelope live at the edge of the Serengeti plain.*

The Mother Leaves Her Young

As soon as the mother is sure that her young can survive alone, she will leave them. This usually happens when cubs are about 16 to 18 months old. They may have killed a prey animal and eaten their fill. Then suddenly, their mother is no longer there. For a while, sisters and brothers will stay together. But then they go their separate ways. Only males stay in a group, living and hunting together.

Friends and Enemies

The cheetah family lives in a paradise for animals. In Serengeti National Park, elephants are the biggest animals of all. Elephants rarely roam through the grasses, but they can pose a danger to cheetah cubs. If a mother cheetah hides her babies in the grass, an elephant could step on the cubs and kill them.

Above: *Zebras are too big for cheetahs, but the cubs still try to hunt them. After many failures, they realize they are only wasting strength.*

Right: *Many colorful birds—including this species, or type, of stork—live in the Serengeti.*

Opposite page: *African elephants are the largest land mammals on earth.*

40

Cheetahs must also be on the lookout for lions, leopards, and hyenas. These predators, animals that hunt other animals, are stronger than cheetahs. But usually only careless or young cheetahs have to fear these enemies.

Adult cheetahs are, after all, the fastest animals on land. As long as they can see danger in time, they can outrun predators.

The lion (above) *is the cheetah's most dangerous enemy.* Hyenas (below, right) *can harm young cheetahs.*

Farewell to the Cheetahs

After 17 weeks, I had to return to my own home. It was time to leave my cheetah family. We had grown so used to each other that leaving was very hard. The cheetahs seemed to be sad. And I was, too.

My time with the cats was wonderful. I got to know the magnificent Serengeti plain, along with a family of wild cheetahs. As I drove away, I thought to myself: "My cheetah family, I love you!"

Right: *A leopard watches from a tree.*
Below: *Thomson's gazelles are frequent prey for cheetahs.*

Cheetah Facts & Figures

No other animal on land is as fast as the cheetah. It reaches speeds of up to 70 miles per hour and can go from a standing start to 45 miles per hour in just two seconds. Compare that to a racehorse—which can gallop at just over 40 miles per hour—or to a human, whose top speed is between 20 and 27 miles per hour.

Although it's fast enough to outrun most predators, the cheetah is an endangered species. The lands where cheetahs live are shrinking. Each year, humans take more and more land for farming. Cheetahs are protected from hunters, but some people still hunt and kill the animals. Fewer than 12,500 of the big cats remain in the wild.

What can you do to help preserve cheetahs? Take a look at the Websites and write to the addresses listed below. And learn more about cheetahs by reading more books about these beautiful cats.

Websites

http://www.cheetah.org
> The Website of the Cheetah Conservation Fund is dedicated to protecting and preserving the big cats.

http://www.defenders.org/cheeta.html
> Check out information about cheetahs at the Website of Defenders of Wildlife, a conservation group.

Organizations

African Wildlife Foundation
1717 Massachusetts Avenue NW
Washington, DC 20036

Cheetah Conservation Fund
c/o The WILD Foundation
P.O. Box 1380
Ojai, CA 93024

Books

Esbensen, Barbara Juster. *Swift as the Wind: The Cheetah.* New York: Orchard Books, 1996.

MacMillan, Dianne M. *Cheetahs.* Minneapolis: Carolrhoda Books, Inc., 1997.

Thompson, Sharon Elaine. *Built for Speed: The Extraordinary, Enigmatic Cheetah.* Minneapolis: Lerner Publications, 1998.

Index

cheetahs: claws, 18, 32, 35; dangers or threats to, 31, 40, 45; eyesight, 12, 31; fear of cars and trucks, 10, 15, 32; hiding of young, 10, 12, 13, 40; learning by playing, 20, 21–22, 27; learning from mother, 20, 26, 27; separation from mother, 39; speed, 18, 41, 45; tails, 24; travel, 10, 12, 15, 16, 24, 31, 36; washing, 29. *See also* drinking, eating, hunting

drinking, 30–31
dry season, 10, 30

eating, 12, 28–29
elephants, 10, 40

food. *See* eating

gazelles, 26, 27
giraffes, 10

hunting, 12, 16, 21, 24, 26–27, 28, 29, 32, 35, 36, 39
hyenas, 29, 41

leopards, 10, 41
lions, 10, 41

predators, 41
prey, 21, 27, 28, 31, 36, 39

rains, 10, 30
rhinoceroses, 10

Serengeti National Park, 10, 12, 16, 24, 31, 40, 43
Serengeti plain. *See* Serengeti National Park

Tanzania, Africa, 10

water, 30–31
weather. *See* dry season, rains

zebras, 10

Metric Conversion Chart		
When You Know:	*Multiply by:*	*To Find:*
yards	0.9	meters
miles	1.6	kilometers
square miles	2.6	square kilometers

173 2839

j599.74   Barfuss, Matto H.
BAR
          My cheetah family.

$22.60

DATE			